Author of Dream Real and
Reflections
Eugene Napoleon

Reflections 2.0

A book of motivational and
comprehensive quotes to
influence positive change.

By

Eugene Napoleon

Reflections 2.0 Credit page

Photo and cover design courtesy of
I Luv That Photo LLC
Tracy Tate

Dedication

"When I take a moment to reflect on my life, I am reminded of the many blessings that came with life experiences. I think of my parents. My mother and father gave me the foundation and the necessary tools in order to be successful in my future endeavors. I am grateful to my mother for her unconditional love and strong faith. The foundation of faith, morals, character, values, discipline and the ability to stand strong on my principles are all lessons I learned from my beloved mother. May she continue to rest in peace."

"I am grateful to God for his patience and grace on my life. I am thankful to my family and friends for their support over the years in every aspect of my life from sports to business. Thank you to those many individuals that had a hand in shaping me and helping me on my continued journey. I am appreciative and humbled."

"To my beautiful and talented wife Tracey, thank you for being my everything. Our marriage is a blessing from God. I am grateful to share my life and experiences with you. I am looking forward to spending the rest of our lives together. I love you more than words can say."

"To my son Brandon. When God blesses parents with children, you can only hope your child will walk the path of being a good human being and follow the teachings of his or her parents in a positive and productive manner. I am extremely proud of the man, the son, the husband and father that you have become. I thank God for you. Be sure to continue to walk in your purpose. I love you to the moon and back."

Reflections 2.0

Table of Contents

CHAPTER 1

THE POWER OF PERSPECTIVE AND WORDS: 10 QUOTES

1. "Emotions are always trapped in the words that are spoken."

2. "Words reflect powerful feelings that can impact decisions."

3. "Honesty is important, be truthful with your words, intentions and actions."

4. "Sometimes nonverbal communication speaks louder than words."

5. "A simple smile can speak a million words."

6. "Body language will show you a lot about people."

7. "Be true to yourself, so you can be true to others."

8. "The mirror will show you many things about yourself."

9. "Your silence has the potential to impact others."

10. "If you speak less, that provides an opportunity to become a better listener."

CHAPTER 2
EFFORT: 10 QUOTES

11. "Your work ethic has no time limit."

12. "Success has more to do with personal effort than overall talent."

13. "Be more about action than words."

14. "Effort starts when you wake up and ends when you decide to no longer work hard."

15. "Your words mean nothing without the effort to complete the task."

16. "Show me a person with great effort and I will show you a successful person."

17. "Discipline, planning and focus equals a positive outcome."

18. "In order to maintain success, it has to be built on the foundation of effort."

19. "While everyone else is talking, just keep moving forward in your purpose."

20. "Be driven by effort and be the author of your own success."

CHAPTER 3
GOALS: 10 QUOTES

21. "The goals you set have to start with your ability to dream big and the determination to work towards those goals."

22. "Greatness and success on any level, will never be obtained without preparation."

23. "Believe in yourself with every step you take."

24. "Be driven by the work it takes to be successful and the end results will be positive."

25. "Only you have a front row seat to your window of success."

26. "Your personal goals are not on public display, stay on your path to achieve them."

27. "If greatness was achieved by only words, everyone would be great."

28. "Take the time to reflect, reset and respond accordingly in the face of adversity."

29. "Goals are set and written on paper, but those goals can only be accomplished with consistent actions."

30. "Achieving goals and success is one thing, sustaining it is something different."

CHAPTER 4
IMPACT: 10 QUOTES

31. "Impact starts with learning from your own downfalls and being willing to share those experiences with others."

32. "Success and failure are related. It's all about understanding and perspective."

33. "Be positive in your intentions and purposeful in your actions."

34. "Commitment starts in the heart."

35. "The positive influence of diversity provides meaningful insight to others."

36. "Lead with integrity, not with blind faith."

37. "When your character is not in question, your words are impactful."

38. "If your core is built on morals, values and ethics, your message will last a lifetime."

39. "When you stand on a strong foundation, others will stand with you."

40. "Having a truthful conversation should never be difficult."

CHAPTER 5
BE GREAT: 10 QUOTES

41. "Make sure your efforts are more focused on putting in the work to be great and not on wasting time talking about being great."

42. "When no one else believes in you, that is when you must believe in yourself."

43. "Greatness comes with having faith and knowing that you have something special to offer."

44. "Never allow someone to stop your personal growth on your journey to greatness."

45. "Be motivated to work on yourself daily."

46. "One of the components of being great starts with personal awareness."

47. "Hold yourself to a much higher standard, because others may not."

48. "Your choices now play a major role in your opportunities later."

49. "Be careful with who you share your dreams with, they may not have the same vision that you do."

50. "If you dream it, you are! If you speak it, you are! If you believe it, you are! Go BE GREAT, because You Are!"

CHAPTER 6
LOYALTY: 10 QUOTES

51. "During difficult times, a person's loyalty is seen by their actions."

52. "It's during the darkest times that you will know who is truly in your corner."

53. "Be loyal for the right reasons, not because you think there is something to gain."

54. "Be appreciative of those individuals that do not come with a price tag."

55. "Never compromise your belief system to be part of something fake."

56. "In order to be loyal to someone else, you first have to be loyal to yourself."

57. "In most cases, loyalty is one of the key components and building blocks to any serious relationship."

58. "You will be judged by others on how you deal with adversity during moments of truth."

59. "The circumstances will not change the outcome if you have someone that is loyal to you."

60. "True loyalty is tenable."

CHAPTER 7
POSITIVE ENERGY: 10 QUOTES

61. "I will stay focused. I will commit. I can do all things. I shall succeed!"

62. "We all have the ability to succeed, it comes down to maintaining a positive attitude when being challenged."

63. "I will not complain. I will not fear failure. I will look forward to the work it takes, in order to reach my chosen destination."

64. "Move away from those individuals that give off negative energy, because that's not the direction you're going in."

65. "Allow your positive energy to change the environment around you."

66. "Negativity will never win in the face of positivity."

67. "Never allow someone's negative words to stop you from achieving a positive outcome."

68. "Walk in the confidence knowing that no one will match your energy or your work ethic on the road to success."

69. "Keep your head up and stay focused, don't allow negative people or their issues to take you off your path."

70. "A million words, said a million times, will not stop the positive energy that flows within you."

CHAPTER 8
CRITICAL THINKING: 10 QUOTES

71. "Stop viewing the world through an unclear window, just simply clean the glass for a better view."

72. "When dealing with issues, you have to take responsibility for the role you played."

73. "Understanding is one of the steps to solving a problem."

74. "Don't put yourself in a box, the world is bigger than that and you will miss out on opportunities."

75. "Building for the future actually started when you decided you wanted a future."

76. "Don't allow your emotional state of mind to become your permanent residence."

77. "Thinking before you make decisions will help the final results."

78. "Take control of your feelings and emotions, never give anyone that kind of power over you."

79. "Be at the top of a situation, never at the bottom, it's a different perspective."

80. "Never make a decision in a few seconds that can potentially cost you years."

CHAPTER 9
EXPECTATIONS: 10 QUOTES

81. "Your expectations start with you."

82. "Stop standing in one place, thinking that the world owes you something and start living life with a meaningful purpose."

83. "Write down your blueprint to your future and revisit it every day."

84. "If you're focused and not anxious, your desired outcome will be different."

85. "Stay in your lane and know the speed limit time is relative."

86. "Stop allowing other people to put their unrealistic expectations on you."

87. "If you put in the work to know yourself, you will know exactly what you're capable of."

88. "Why be happy in the top 10, when you've worked to be #1."

89. "Be who you are and not who someone else expects you to be."

90. "No matter what people tell you, your heart knows the truth."

CHAPTER 10
RESPECT: 10 QUOTES

91. "Respect is not just a word it should be the first thing that people say about you."

92. "The way you carry yourself is the way people will treat you."

93. "Love and respect yourself."

94. "Don't allow the disrespectful ways of others to hinder your view of the world."

95. "Be mindful of how you treat others, because it's a reflection of yourself."

96. "If you know the right thing, do the right thing."

97. "Respect brings out many different emotions."

98. "No matter what's going on, it should be handled with respect."

99. "The lack of respect can change things in seconds."

100. "The power of respect can change the world."

About the Author

About The Author: Eugene Napoleon is a two-time Bestselling Author of the books, Dream Real and Reflections. He is a two-time recipient of the Teacher of The Year Award for both Hudson County and Union County School Districts. Napoleon was named the Governor's Teacher of The Year at Soehl Middle School located in Linden, New Jersey for the 2022-2023 school year. Napoleon is extremely committed to giving back to his community and has been a Special Education Teacher for the past 25 years.

Napoleon is the CEO and President of Nap Vision Entertainment and former Professional Football Player in the Arena Football League (AFL) and the Canadian Football League (CFL). Napoleon is from Marion Garden Projects located in Jersey City, New Jersey. He graduated from St. Joseph's of the Palisades high school located in West New York, New Jersey. Eugene was a star football player at St. Joseph's, which lead to him being inducted in the Bluejays Hall of Fame. Napoleon made 7 high school All-American teams and was rank the #1 running back in Hudson County, the 13th best running back in the country and #3 on the East Coast by Tom Lemming, viewed by many as the #1 high school football recruiting analyst in the country. Napoleon is a proud graduate of West Virginia University and was a standout running back during the mid-80's for the Mountaineers. He was honored to play on the 11-0 undefeated Mountaineers football team that played the University of Notre Dame for the 1988 National Championship in the Fiesta Bowl. Napoleon talks about his college football career and experiences at WVU in the documentary Inside the Jersey, which is streaming on several platforms.

Napoleon has successfully been in the music and sports entertainment industries for over 27 years. He is personally involved with marketing, promotions, contract negotiations, special events, camps and clinics, speaking engagements, endorsement opportunities, consultant work along with film and documentaries.

"Having a great work ethic provides many future opportunities."

"Life is all about perspective and inspiring positive change in the life of others."

CPSIA information can be obtained
at www.ICGtesting.com
Printed in the USA
BVHW041707240523
664816BV00017B/154